ECHOES *of* LIFE

*A Singer's Journey of **Love**, **Loss**, and **Triumph***

ARCHANA MEHROTRA

ISBN
Paperback 979-8-89777-950-5
Hardcase 979-8-89929-703-8

To My Pillars of Strength…

This work is dedicated to two remarkable men who have shaped my life in profound and meaningful ways: my late father and my dear brother.

To my father: You were the cornerstone of my life. Your love, wisdom, and values formed the foundation upon which I have built everything I am today. Your strength, integrity, and guidance continue to inspire me, even though you are no longer with us. I carry your lessons with me every day, and I strive to honor your memory in everything I do. Your legacy lives on, not just in the words you shared, but in the quiet strength you instilled in me. I miss you deeply, but your spirit will forever guide me.

To my brother: You are my constant support, my greatest ally, and a true source of inspiration. Your love, encouragement, and understanding have meant the world to me. We have shared countless moments of joy and challenge, and I am incredibly grateful to have you by my side. Your strength and unwavering belief in me continue to lift me, and your presence fills my life with purpose and light. I am so proud of the person you are and the brother you have always been.

To My Mother: you are my support system. Your unwavering love, strength, and encouragement have been a constant source of comfort and inspiration. I am so fortunate to have you by my side, and I will always be grateful for everything you do. Thank you for being my rock.

I want to extend my special gratitude **to Pearl, Pari,** and my entire family for being my unwavering backbone. Your love, support, and belief in me have given me the strength to face every challenge. I am truly blessed to have such an incredible family by my side. Thank you from the bottom of my heart

Table of Contents

Foreword   *7*

Chapter 1   Beginnings   9

Chapter 2   The Path to Education   13

Chapter 3   The Family Legacy   18

Chapter 4   Overcoming Obstacles   22

Chapter 5   Finding Purpose   26

Chapter 6   Triumphs and Milestones   30

Chapter 7   The Impact of Loss   34

Chapter 8   Relationships and Friendships   37

Chapter 9   A Life of Learning and Growth   40

Chapter 10   My Philosophy and Values   44

Chapter 11   Parth – The Light of My Life   49

Chapter 12   A Tribute to My Father   53

Chapter 13   To the Heart That Raised Me –
             My Mother   56

Chapter 14   My Journey   61

Chapter 15   The Strength of My Journey – Parth   66

Chapter 16   Hearing Journey of Path   70

Chapter 17 A Mother's Fight   75

Chapter 18 Looking Ahead   78

Expressions of Gratitude   83

Foreword

It is said that the journey of a thousand miles begins with a single step, but some journeys are not just about the steps we take but also about the stories we leave behind. The story you are about to read is one of resilience, love, and the incredible human spirit that refuses to give up, no matter the hurdles life places in our path. This autobiography is not merely a recount of events; it is a celebration of a life filled with moments of joy, sorrow, growth, and unwavering strength.

As I reflect on my own journey, I find that it is the people who have shaped me—those who walked beside me, those who lifted me when I stumbled, and those whose memories continue to inspire me—that define my path. This book is a tribute to them. It is a dedication to my father, who instilled in me the values that continue to guide my every decision, and to my brother, whose support and encouragement have been a constant throughout my life. It is also dedicated to my son, Parth, whose innocence and energy remind me daily of the beauty and promise of the future.

Life, with all its complexities, teaches us the importance of understanding our past, embracing the present, and looking forward to what lies ahead. Through these pages, I invite you to walk with me, to experience the triumphs and the heartaches, the challenges and the celebrations, that have shaped me into who I am today. It is my hope that in sharing my story, you may find something that resonates with your own journey, something that inspires you to move forward with courage and conviction, no matter where life may take you.

With each chapter, I offer a window into my world—a world that continues to evolve, driven by the lessons of the past and the dreams of the future. I am grateful for every step I have taken, for every person I have encountered, and for the love and strength that have propelled me forward. And as I share my journey with you, I do so with the belief that our stories, in their most authentic form, have the power to connect, heal, and inspire.

Thank you for reading and for allowing me the opportunity to share this part of my life with you.

Chapter 1

Beginnings

Every journey has its roots, and mine began in a small but vibrant world, where dreams were nurtured and the foundation for my future was laid. Born into a family that valued hard work, integrity, and love, my early years were filled with moments that have stayed with me, shaping the person I would become. Looking back, I realize how much these formative years defined not only the path I would walk but also the values that would guide me along the way.

I grew up in a home where family was everything. My father, Shri Laxmi Nath Mehrotra, a man of quiet strength, was the younger of his siblings and served as a pillar of wisdom for us all. Though he may have been the younger brother among his siblings, his character shone brightly, guiding not only his family but also those around him. His life was marked by deep respect for his elders and a steady presence that carried with it a quiet, yet profound, influence. My father's role in our family extended beyond that of a mere provider; he was the steady hand that helped us navigate through life's ups and downs.

My father instilled in me a simple but powerful philosophy: "Live with integrity, work with dedication, and always treat others with respect." These words remain etched in my heart, and I carry them with me every day.

Even though my father is no longer with us, his teachings continue to guide me, helping me navigate life's challenges with grace and resilience.

As the second child in our family, I was fortunate to have the love and support of my parents and siblings. We were five in total—four sisters, including me, and one brother. Sadly, two of my sisters are no longer with us, and their loss has left a void in my heart. Their memories, however, continue to live on within me, reminding me of the importance of family and the deep connections we share.

Growing up in Lucknow, a city rich in history and culture, I was surrounded by influences that shaped not just my academic path but my worldview. The values of tradition, respect for elders, and the pursuit of knowledge were instilled in me from an early age. My parents were not just providers, they were my first teachers, showing me the value of learning and the importance of being true to oneself.

In my school years, I developed a deep thirst for knowledge and a curiosity that would guide me throughout my life. It was not just about academics; it was about asking questions, seeking answers, and growing through the process. The encouragement from my teachers and the support of my family helped me understand that learning was not limited to textbooks—it was a lifelong journey of self-improvement.

My father always emphasized the importance of education. He believed that success was not just about academic achievements but about building character, resilience, and a deep respect for others. His belief in the power of knowledge and personal growth shaped my own approach to life and learning.

It was through his guidance that I learned to value the process of learning and the impact it has on shaping our lives.

The challenges I faced growing up only strengthened my resolve. Whether it was overcoming personal obstacles or facing moments of doubt, I learned that success is not just about reaching a destination but about persevering through adversity. It was through these trials that I understood the true meaning of resilience and the importance of maintaining integrity, no matter the circumstances.

Reflecting on these early years, I realize how much they laid the groundwork for who I would become. My father's life, the teachings of my mother, and the lessons from my teachers and community all contributed to the foundation on which my future would be built. These early moments were not just a beginning; they were the pillars that would support everything that came after.

The warmth of family gatherings, the wisdom of my father, the love of my mother, and the support of my siblings—these memories continue to guide me as I take the next steps on my journey. They are the compass that directs my path, reminding me of the importance of family, integrity, and the pursuit of knowledge. As I move forward in life, I carry these values with me, honoring the lessons of the past while embracing the challenges and opportunities of the future.

Chapter 2

The Path to Education

Education has always been more than just a means to an end for me—it has been a journey of self-discovery, empowerment, and transformation. The path I embarked upon in the pursuit of knowledge was not always smooth or predictable, but it was one that shaped my values, my ambitions, and my identity.

From a young age, I was aware of the importance of education. My parents, especially my father, placed great emphasis on learning, not just in terms of academic success but as a way of enriching one's life and understanding the world. I remember his words echoing in my mind: "Knowledge is the key that opens every door." These words guided me through the early years of my academic journey and gave me the strength to face challenges, whether big or small.

Growing up in Lucknow, I attended Mahila Degree College, where I completed my B.Sc. The experience was not just about attending classes; it was about cultivating a

curiosity for the world around me. My teachers at college were not just educators; they were mentors who ignited in me a love for learning.

They encouraged me to ask questions, think critically, and explore beyond the confines of textbooks. It was during these years that I truly began to appreciate the power of knowledge, not just as a tool for professional success, but a means of shaping my worldview.

The transition from school to college was not without its challenges. As a second child in a family with five siblings, I had to balance the expectations of my family, the responsibilities at home, and my academic pursuits. The support of my parents, especially my father, was invaluable during this time. He never placed unrealistic demands on me, but instead encouraged me to follow my passion and strive for excellence in everything I did. His belief in me helped me navigate the pressures of academia and family responsibilities.

As I moved forward in my education, I felt the pull of something greater than just completing a degree. I wanted to contribute to society, to make a meaningful impact, and to use the skills I was developing to help others. It was this sense of purpose that led me to pursue certifications that would complement my academic background. I completed the HSM certification from NIIT Lucknow, a step that helped me develop important skills in management and leadership. This was just the beginning of my exploration into areas beyond traditional education, as I continued to seek opportunities that would allow me to broaden my horizons and contribute in new ways.

One of the most pivotal moments in my educational journey came when I decided to pursue an MBA in Finance and Accounting from Amity University Online. Currently, as I continue to study this program, I am gaining a deeper understanding of finance and business—skills that will not only enhance my career but also equip me with the knowledge to make informed decisions, both personally and professionally. The MBA has also opened my eyes to the world of digital marketing, an area that blends strategy, creativity, and technology.

This shift into digital marketing became a key focus as I realized the power of online platforms in shaping business and communication in the modern world.

The pursuit of education has never been about following a prescribed path for me. It has always been about exploring new territories, pushing boundaries, and embracing the unknown. I realized that learning does not end with formal education—it is a continuous process that extends beyond classrooms and degrees. This realization became even more apparent as I started to explore the world of digital marketing and online platforms. I earned a certificate in Digital Marketing, which allowed me to merge my academic background with my growing interest in the digital world.

Throughout my journey, I was fortunate to be part of communities and networks that encouraged learning and growth. My involvement with IKMG, for instance, allowed me to combine my skills with my passion for writing, giving me an avenue to contribute to the IKMG magazine and radio. The experience of writing and creating content for a global audience further fueled my desire to expand my knowledge and share it with others. The lessons I learned through these experiences, both in formal education and outside it, shaped my career and my approach to life.

As I reflect on my path to education, I realize that it has been far from conventional. There have been twists and turns, moments of uncertainty, and plenty of obstacles. Yet, each step has been a learning experience that has contributed to my growth. Education, for me, has never been a destination but a journey—a journey that has empowered me to chase my dreams, take risks, and ultimately become the person I am today.

The lessons I learned through my educational experiences have not only shaped my career but also my values and perspective on life. I learned the importance of perseverance, adaptability, and continuous growth. But most of all, I learned that education is a lifelong pursuit—one that has no end, but only new beginnings. It is the foundation upon which I continue to build, as I embrace the opportunities that lie ahead and remain committed to learning, growing, and contributing to the world around me.

The Family Legacy

The origins of my family's legacy are deeply rooted in the combined efforts of both my father and mother, each contributing their own unique strengths to create a foundation that continues to guide us today. Their lives were intertwined with a shared vision of hard work, resilience, and service to others. While my father was the driving force behind our family's business in fragrance, my mother has been equally influential in shaping the values that have defined our home and family life. Her presence remains a strong guiding force in our lives today.

My father's journey in the perfume industry began in the 1970s and 1980s, a time when perfumery was a largely unexplored field in India. He was a pioneer in the industry, venturing into a business that required not only technical expertise but also immense perseverance. Despite limited resources and a developing market, my father worked tirelessly to create exquisite fragrances that would eventually earn global recognition. He faced many challenges—financial instability, fierce competition, and market limitations—but his determination never wavered. Slowly, his hard work paid off. Over time, he built a name for himself, with renowned brands worldwide seeking his expertise in fragrance design.

But the success of my father was not just in his ability to build a business from the ground up; it was also his unwavering dedication to giving back to the community. His philanthropic nature was evident in his efforts to support local causes, from providing food and shelter to the underprivileged to contributing generously to local temples. His acts of kindness were deeply ingrained in his character and became a cornerstone of our family values. It was this generosity that not only made him a respected figure in the business world but also a beloved member of the community.

Though my father is no longer with us, his legacy continues to live on. My mother, a strong and loving figure, remains the heart of our family, keeping alive the values that my father instilled in us. She has continued to guide us with love, wisdom, and a strong sense of responsibility. While my father was the face of the business, it was my mother who ensured that we remained grounded as a family. Her unwavering support, both for my father and for us as children, kept our lives balanced and filled with love.

My mother's role in our family's legacy is vital. She was the pillar of support during the years when my father was building the business. Her strength and quiet determination kept the family united, even during difficult times. She balanced the challenges of raising children and managing the household while supporting my father's work. Beyond that, my mother continued to carry forward the values that both she and my father held dear: hard work, perseverance, compassion, and community service.

She continues to live by these principles today, offering her wisdom and support to our family and to those in need.

Together, my parents built a legacy that extended beyond the success of the fragrance business. They created a family culture based on resilience, dedication, and giving back. While my father laid the foundation for the business, it was my mother's nurturing spirit and moral compass that kept our family connected to its core values. They were partners in every sense, and their collective efforts made our family legacy one of hard work, generosity, and love.

Today, I carry forward the lessons they taught me, passing them on to my own children. The values of hard work, compassion, and community responsibility continue to guide our family. My mother's presence today reminds us that the family legacy is not just a thing of the past but an ongoing commitment to love, integrity, and service. Through her continued influence, our family's story will carry on, and the lessons of resilience, kindness, and generosity will continue to inspire future generations.

In reflecting on my family's legacy, I see that the most important things my parents have passed down are not material wealth or success but the values and principles that guided their lives. This is the true inheritance we carry forward—one of love, respect, and a commitment to helping others. It is a legacy I hope to nurture, just as my parents have done for me, and to pass on to my children. Through this, their influence will endure, not just in the business they built, but in the hearts of those they have touched.

Chapter 4

Overcoming Obstacles

Life has a way of throwing challenges at us when we least expect them, and often, it is during these times of turmoil that our true strength emerges. My journey as a single parent began with a heartbreak that changed my life forever. Parth was born prematurely, and his fragile condition left doctors uncertain about his survival. The uncertainty and fear were overwhelming, but amidst this emotional storm, another devastating blow hit me—Parth's father left us, unable to shoulder the responsibility of this difficult situation. His departure marked the beginning of a life where I had to navigate uncharted waters as both a mother and a source of unwavering strength for my child.

In those early days, the fear of losing Parth consumed me. Every moment spent caring for him was filled with prayers, silent tears, and a determination that grew stronger with every passing day. I found myself constantly asking questions I didn't have answers to: *How would I provide for him? How would I raise him alone?* But even in the darkest of times, life has a way of showing us glimmers of hope. My father and brother stepped in as my anchors, offering me unconditional support. They ensured that I never had to worry about finances or managing the overwhelming responsibilities of this new reality. Their unwavering encouragement reminded me that, while Parth's father might have left, I was far from alone.

Caring for Parth became my sole focus. Every small milestone he achieved felt monumental—the warmth of his tiny fingers gripping mine, the faintest flicker of recognition in his eyes, the gradual improvements in his health. Each of these moments filled my heart with hope and strengthened my resolve. My father and brother were not just my financial supporters; they were my emotional pillars. They ensured that our home was a haven of love and support, and their presence filled the void left by his father's absence.

As Parth grew older, the challenges evolved but never diminished. There were countless sleepless nights, doctor visits, and emotional hurdles. Through it all, I learned to find strength in the love that surrounded us. My brother became a father figure to Parth, showering him with affection and wisdom. My father's role as a grandfather went far beyond tradition—he became a mentor and a source of inspiration for Parth. Their involvement didn't just lighten my burden; it showed me that family could fill the gaps left by life's adversities.

Parth's journey from a fragile newborn to a determined young man has been nothing short of extraordinary. Despite his rocky start, he grew up to be resilient, curious, and passionate about life. Watching him pursue his dreams was like witnessing a miracle unfold. When he graduated with a Bachelor of Journalism & Mass Communication from Amity University Lucknow, it was a moment of immense pride. I wasn't just proud of him for his achievements; I was proud of the strength and courage we both exhibited to reach that milestone. His success was a shared victory—a testament to the power of love, perseverance, and familial bonds.

The absence of Parth's father was undeniably painful, but it taught us invaluable lessons. It showed us that strength doesn't always come from those we expect; sometimes, it comes from within and from those who step up when others step away. My father and brother's unwavering support created a nurturing environment where Parth could thrive. Their love made up for everything we had lost and more. It also taught Parth the value of family and resilience, qualities that I see in him every day.

In society, being a single parent often comes with its own set of challenges and judgments. There's a pervasive mindset that single parents are somehow incomplete or struggling more than others. People tend to view a single parent as someone who is "doing it alone," often with an unspoken sense of pity or doubt about their ability to manage. There were moments when I could feel the weight of these societal expectations and stereotypes, particularly as a woman raising a child alone. Some would question how I managed without a partner, and some even implied that my son might somehow be missing out on the "complete" family structure. But I refused to let society's narrow view define our reality. The truth is, the absence of a father figure didn't diminish Parth's potential or my ability to provide a nurturing environment. Instead, it showed me that strength doesn't come from the expectations of others, but from within, and from the unwavering love and commitment that a parent can offer. I have learned that what matters most is the love and support we give each other, not how others perceive our family.

Today, as I reflect on this chapter of our lives, I realize that overcoming obstacles isn't just about surviving hardships—it's about thriving despite them. It's about finding joy in the little victories, leaning on the support of loved ones, and building a life that defies the odds. Our story is a reminder that love, in its truest form, has the power to heal even the deepest wounds.

Parth's journey continues to inspire me, and I am grateful for the family that stood by us during the toughest times. This chapter is not just about the obstacles we faced but about the triumphs we achieved together as a family. It is a celebration of resilience, love, and the unyielding strength that binds us all.

Chapter 5

Finding Purpose

Finding purpose is not always a linear journey, and for me, it was something that unfolded over time, through experiences, and in moments of both triumph and adversity. For years, I focused on surviving the challenges of life, taking care of my family, and ensuring that Parth had the best chance at life after everything we had been through. But as time passed, I realized that simply moving through life wasn't enough; I needed to find something deeper—a reason, a calling that gave meaning to the struggles and sacrifices I had made.

After Parth's premature birth, I began to truly reflect on the direction my life was taking. Becoming a single parent wasn't a decision, but a reality that was thrust upon me, and it came with a deep emotional and financial toll. Yet, it also instilled in me a relentless sense of resilience. While society's expectations and judgments weighed on me, I realized that my purpose wasn't to live up to their standards but to carve my own path, one that would not only provide for my son but also allow me to grow as a person. In the face of adversity, I saw an opportunity to redefine my life on my terms, and it was from this place of strength that I began to discover my true purpose.

The first part of this journey was about healing, and healing began with self-compassion. I stopped seeing myself through the lens of others' judgment and started to understand my worth. I also realized that my purpose didn't only have to be about being a mother; it was about reclaiming my dreams, passions, and aspirations. I had always been interested in the art of fragrance and the power of storytelling. My family's legacy in perfume-making ignited a spark in me that had been dimmed over the years. I had a wealth of knowledge, both from my father's experiences and my own passions, and it became clear to me that I could contribute to the world by bringing my unique perspective to these areas. It wasn't just about the business of fragrances; it was about creating something that resonated with people—connecting them to memories, emotions, and experiences through the sense of smell and storytelling.

As I ventured into the world of blogging, I began to realize how much I enjoyed sharing my thoughts, experiences, and insights with others. Writing became an outlet for me to express the internal transformations I was going through. I found that sharing my personal journey of motherhood, resilience, and self-discovery resonated with readers. It wasn't just about words on a page; it was about creating an impact, inspiring others who may have faced similar challenges. In each blog post, I was not only documenting my experiences but also helping others feel seen, heard, and understood.

Alongside this, my involvement with organizations like IKMG allowed me to extend my purpose into the community. I learned that giving back was just as important as any personal success. My father's legacy of kindness and service had always been at the core of our family values, and as I gave more of myself to these causes, I felt a deep sense of fulfillment. I began to see that my purpose wasn't about achieving conventional success or meeting others' expectations—it was about finding joy in the small moments, contributing to the well-being of others, and continuing the legacy of love, service, and compassion that my family had taught me.

Through these various avenues, I started to uncover the layers of my purpose. It wasn't confined to a single role or achievement; it was about embracing the fullness of who I am. It was about balancing my role as a mother with my passions, my work, and my ability to serve others. I realized that purpose doesn't just come from one thing—it comes from the alignment of your values, your passions, and your actions.

Finding purpose has been an ongoing process, one that I continue to explore and refine. I now know that purpose is not a destination, but a journey. It's the everyday decisions, the challenges you overcome, and the way you contribute to the world that define it. It is something that continually evolves as you grow. And in embracing this, I've found peace and fulfillment in knowing that no matter the obstacles I face, I am living a life that is meaningful—not just to me, but to the world around me.

Every day, I remind myself that purpose is about connecting with what truly matters: to love deeply, to give freely, and to live with intention. And through this journey, I have learned to embrace my role in the world with pride, knowing that the path I am on is one that brings purpose to my life and to those I touch.

Chapter 6

Triumphs and Milestones

In life, triumphs and milestones are not always measured by grand achievements or societal accolades, but often by the quiet victories that emerge from perseverance, resilience, and an unwavering belief in oneself. For me, each step forward, each obstacle overcome, has been a triumph in its own right. As I reflect on the journey I've traveled, I realize that the true measure of success lies not in the recognition of others but in the fulfillment of personal goals and the lessons learned along the way.

The first significant milestone came when Parth, against all odds, not only survived his premature birth but thrived. When doctors had warned us of the slim chances for his survival, I remember feeling a wave of helplessness wash over me. I had no idea what the future would hold, and it was a terrifying thought. But through the countless sleepless nights, the hospital visits, and the endless worry, I also witnessed a strength in my son that I had never anticipated. Parth defied every expectation, proving that determination and love could overcome even the toughest of circumstances. Watching him grow into the intelligent, driven young man he is today—having completed his Bachelor's in Journalism & Mass Communication from Amity University—is a triumph that fills my heart with pride. It is not just his academic achievement that stands as a testament to our collective strength, but his resilience in facing the challenges of life head-on. Parth's success is my success, and every step he takes toward his dreams feels like a milestone we've crossed together.

Another significant triumph was my ability to redefine my life after becoming a single mother. When Parth's father left us, the weight of that abandonment was immense, and the road ahead seemed impossibly long. It wasn't just about being a single parent; it was about rebuilding my entire life and sense of self. It took time, and at moments, it felt like I was walking through darkness without any clear direction. But I made a conscious decision not to let this hardship define me. Instead of succumbing to the overwhelming challenges, I chose to rise above them. I found my voice and used it to carve out a new path—one that included professional growth, personal development, and, most importantly, a sense of peace with the life I was creating. I returned to my education, pursued new interests, and began contributing more to my community. These choices were the small yet powerful triumphs that marked the beginning of my transformation.

One of the proudest moments came when I embraced my writing. Blogging became a therapeutic outlet, a way to channel my thoughts, experiences, and emotions into something meaningful. It wasn't an easy decision, as it meant stepping outside my comfort zone and confronting my vulnerabilities. But as I began to share my story, I found that others resonated with my words, and I realized the power of storytelling. The feedback I received from readers, the sense that my words were impacting others, became a milestone in my personal journey. I had found my purpose, and through writing, I had unlocked a new dimension of myself—one that was both healing and empowering.

In addition to personal triumphs, I also experienced milestones in my professional life. I was fortunate enough to work with the IKMG organization, where I not only contributed as a writer but also took on a leadership role as President. Through this platform, I was able to make a real difference in my community, contribute to meaningful causes, and work alongside like-minded individuals. My journey through IKMG helped me develop leadership skills, a sense of responsibility, and a deeper understanding of what it means to serve others. This professional achievement was a direct reflection of my personal growth, and it marked another milestone in my quest for purpose.

Over the years, I have also managed to stay true to my family's legacy in the fragrance industry. Though I initially felt uncertain about stepping into my father's shoes, I realized that his work was part of me, and his passion for creating beautiful fragrances was something I carried with me. Taking steps to revive and continue his work, while blending it with my own interests and creativity, has been both a tribute to his legacy and a personal triumph. By combining my skills and knowledge, I have found my own voice in the world of fragrance and storytelling. Each step forward in this area has been a celebration of my growth, not just as a businesswoman but as someone who honors the path my family laid out for me.

Milestones in life are often not seen in the moment they occur; it's only in reflection that we realize their significance. For me, the journey from motherhood to self-empowerment, from uncertainty to confidence, is one of quiet yet profound triumphs. Every challenge, every setback, and every victory along the way has shaped me into the person I am today—a woman who has weathered storms and come out stronger on the other side.

As I look back, I see that each of these triumphs and milestones has been a building block that has shaped the life I live now. There are many more to come, and though I know there will be new challenges to face, I also know that I am equipped to handle them with grace and determination. Triumph is not the absence of struggle, but the ability to rise above it. And with every milestone, I am reminded that no matter how difficult the journey may seem, it is always worth it in the end.

Chapter 7

The Impact of Loss

Life is often a journey of triumphs interspersed with moments of deep loss. For me, the journey has been marked by significant heartbreaks that reshaped my perspective and tested my resilience. The loss of my father, the end of my marriage, and the passing of two beloved sisters were profound events that left an indelible mark on my life. Each of these experiences brought a unique kind of pain, yet they also revealed the depth of my strength and my capacity to endure.

The day my father passed away remains etched in my memory as one of the most challenging moments of my life. My father was more than just a parent; he was a pillar of wisdom, strength, and unyielding support. He instilled in me values that continue to guide me—dedication to one's purpose, compassion for others, and the belief that with hard work, anything is possible. When he left us, it felt as though the foundation of my world had crumbled. I missed his voice, his advice, and the comforting reassurance that he was always there for me. Yet, in the midst of this profound loss, I realized that his teachings were not lost—they lived on within me. My father's legacy became my anchor, a constant reminder to uphold his values and continue the journey he started.

The end of my marriage was another pivotal moment of loss in my life. It was not just the dissolution of a relationship but the unraveling of dreams and a shared future. When Parth was born prematurely, it was a testing time for both of us. While I embraced the challenges with the fierce determination of a mother, his father chose to walk away, leaving us to navigate the difficulties alone. The pain of his departure was amplified by the judgments of society, which often casts a critical eye on single mothers. However, rather than succumbing to despair, I chose to rebuild my life with dignity and purpose. I realized that my son deserved a stable, loving environment, and I was determined to provide it, no matter the obstacles.

Losing two of my sisters was another chapter of profound grief. Sisters are the companions of your soul, the ones who share your secrets, dreams, and laughter. Their absence created a void that no one else could fill. The memories of our shared childhood, the laughter we exchanged, and the love we held for each other became bittersweet treasures. Their passing reminded me of the fragility of life and the importance of cherishing every moment with loved ones. The grief I felt was overwhelming, but it also deepened my empathy and my resolve to create joyful memories with those who remain.

Amid these losses, I was fortunate to have the unwavering support of my family. My mother, with her quiet strength, became a source of comfort and wisdom. My brother stood by me, not only emotionally but also financially, ensuring that I could focus on healing and raising Parth without additional burdens. Their love and encouragement reminded me that even in the darkest times, the bonds of family provide light and solace.

Society's perception of single parents added another layer of challenge. Often, single mothers are unfairly judged or viewed through a lens of pity. While the stigma could have been a source of discouragement, it instead became a catalyst for my determination. I wanted to prove to myself, my son, and the world that being a single parent is not a limitation but a testament to resilience and strength. Parth's growth, achievements, and happiness became my response to every whispered comment or judgmental glance.

Loss, I have learned, is not an event that can be overcome but a state that one must learn to live with. It teaches us to adapt, to grow, and to cherish what remains. The absence of my father, the challenges of single motherhood, and the grief of losing my sisters have not broken me. Instead, they have given me a deeper appreciation for life's beauty and fragility. These experiences have shaped me into the person I am today—a mother, a daughter, a sister, and, most importantly, a survivor.

The pain of these losses will always be a part of my story, but so will the lessons they brought. They have taught me that love persists even in absence, that resilience can be found in the face of adversity, and that life's meaning lies in the connections we nurture and the legacy we leave behind. My journey is far from over, but I carry with me the strength and wisdom born from these trials, ready to face whatever comes next.

Relationships and Friendships

Relationships and friendships are the intricate threads that weave the fabric of our lives, offering love, companionship, and the shared joy of life's experiences. Over the years, I've come to understand that these connections are not just a source of comfort but also an opportunity for growth and self-discovery. My journey with relationships and friendships has been one of learning, laughter, and, at times, heartbreak, but each experience has left me stronger and wiser.

Friendship has always held a special place in my heart. From my school days to adulthood, I have been fortunate to build lasting bonds with people who have stood by me in moments of joy and sorrow. My friends have been my confidants, my cheerleaders, and my chosen family. Whether it was late-night conversations, shared laughter over silly jokes, or the quiet support during challenging times, my friends have been a constant source of strength and positivity.

One of the most valuable lessons I've

learned about friendship is the importance of mutual respect and understanding. True friendships are built on trust and acceptance, where each person feels seen and valued for who they are. Over time, I have nurtured these relationships with care, always striving to be as supportive to my friends as they have been to me.

However, relationships and friendships are not without their challenges. Life's circumstances sometimes create distances—both physical and emotional—that can strain even the strongest of bonds. There have been moments when misunderstandings and differences threatened to overshadow the connection I shared with someone. These experiences taught me the value of communication and forgiveness. I realized that every relationship requires effort, patience, and the willingness to let go of pride to truly thrive.

In my journey, romantic relationships have been a blend of love and lessons. My marriage, though it ended, taught me profound truths about vulnerability, partnership, and resilience. The dissolution of that bond was a painful chapter, but it also helped me redefine what love means to me. I learned to prioritize self-respect and emotional well-being, understanding that a healthy relationship is one where both individuals grow together without compromising their individuality.

Motherhood brought another layer of depth to my relationships. My bond with Parth is one of the most profound connections I've ever experienced. It's a relationship that has taught me the true meaning of unconditional love, patience, and sacrifice. As a single parent, I've also had the privilege of forming relationships with other mothers who understand the unique challenges and joys of parenting. These connections have provided me with a sense of community and shared understanding that I deeply cherish.

Through the years, I've also come to appreciate the power of kindness and empathy in relationships. People come into our lives for a reason, and every interaction, whether fleeting or lasting, has the potential to teach us something valuable. I've made it a point to approach relationships with an open heart and a willingness to give as much as I receive.

Yet, some friendships and relationships naturally drift apart over time, not because of conflict but due to the changing rhythms of life. This realization was initially painful, but it taught me to value the memories shared and to let go with grace. People who were once integral to my story have left their mark, and for that, I am grateful.

The relationships I have today are a testament to the resilience and beauty of human connection. My friends are my anchor, my family is my foundation, and every bond I share is a reflection of the love and care I strive to nurture in my life. These relationships are my reminder that no matter the trials we face, the connections we build with others are what make life meaningful and fulfilling.

As I continue my journey, I remain committed to valuing the relationships that enrich my life. Whether it's through a kind word, a thoughtful gesture, or simply being present, I believe in the power of connection to heal, inspire, and uplift. My relationships and friendships are not just chapters in my story; they are the essence of the life I have lived and the legacy I hope to leave behind.

Chapter 9

A Life of Learning and Growth

Life is a continuous journey of learning and growth, a path where every experience shapes us into a more refined version of ourselves. My life, too, has been a testament to this principle, with each phase offering lessons that have broadened my perspective, strengthened my character, and deepened my understanding of the world.

Education, both formal and informal, has played a significant role in my journey. From my foundational years of schooling to my pursuit of higher education, I have always believed in the transformative power of knowledge. My academic journey, which includes earning a B.Sc. and advancing to an MBA in Finance and Accounting, reflects my commitment to personal and professional growth. These milestones were not just about acquiring degrees but about embracing the discipline, perseverance, and curiosity that come with the process of learning.

However, some of the most profound lessons I've learned didn't come from books or classrooms but from the challenges life presented. The hurdles of single parenthood, the loss of loved ones, and the need to rebuild my life after significant setbacks taught me resilience and adaptability. Each trial was a teacher in its own right, imparting wisdom that no structured curriculum ever could. I learned the importance of self-reliance, the value of hope, and the necessity of embracing change with courage.

Personal growth is not limited to overcoming difficulties; it also flourishes in moments of joy and discovery. My creative pursuits, such as writing, singing, and contributing to community initiatives, have been avenues of immense personal development. These activities allowed me to express myself, connect with others, and contribute meaningfully to the world around me. They have helped me understand the significance of nurturing my passions alongside fulfilling my responsibilities.

As a mother, I've had the privilege of witnessing growth through a different lens. Raising my son, Parth, has been a journey of mutual learning. His curiosity and enthusiasm for life have been a constant reminder to embrace each day with wonder and an open heart.

Through him, I've relearned the importance of adaptability, patience, and the boundless potential of a curious mind.

Another cornerstone of my growth has been the relationships I've built along the way. Friends, mentors, and family members have been my guides, offering insights and support that have propelled me forward. These connections have taught me the value of collaboration, the strength of shared experiences, and the power of kindness.

In the professional realm, I've continuously sought opportunities to expand my skills and expertise. Whether through certifications, digital marketing, or research work, I've strived to stay relevant in an ever-evolving world. This pursuit of excellence has not only enriched my career but has also instilled a deep sense of accomplishment and self-worth.

Spiritual growth, too, has been an integral part of my journey. Life's adversities have often nudged me toward introspection, helping me understand the importance of inner peace and faith. Whether through meditation, prayer, or simply spending quiet moments in nature, I've learned to cultivate a sense of balance and gratitude, which has been a source of strength during challenging times.

Looking back, I realize that growth is not about perfection but about progress. It's about taking each step with purpose, learning from missteps, and celebrating even the smallest victories. My journey is far from over, and there's so much more to learn, explore, and achieve.

As I continue to move forward, I remain committed to a life of learning and growth. The world is a vast classroom, and every day offers a new lesson. I embrace this with open arms, knowing that the pursuit of knowledge and self-improvement is not just a path but a way of life.

My Philosophy and Values

At the core of who I am lies a set of deeply held beliefs and values that have shaped my journey and continue to guide me through life's most challenging and joyful moments. These guiding principles are not just abstract ideas; they are the foundation on which I build every decision, relationship, and endeavor. They are the compass that directs me toward growth, compassion, and purpose.

1. Resilience in the Face of Adversity

Life is full of unexpected turns—some joyous, others heart-wrenching. But it is our response to adversity that defines us. Through my personal experiences of loss, divorce, and the challenges of single parenthood, I have learned that resilience is the key to overcoming even the most difficult times. Rather than succumbing to despair, I've adopted a mindset of perseverance. I believe that no matter how insurmountable a challenge may seem, there is always a way forward, a lesson to learn, and strength to gain from each hardship. This resilience is not about denying pain but acknowledging it and choosing to keep moving forward, with hope and determination.

2. The Power of Compassion and Empathy

One of the values I hold most dearly is compassion—both for others and for myself. Having faced personal struggles,

I am acutely aware of the importance of empathy. Compassion allows us to connect with others on a deeper level, to truly understand their pain, joy, and struggles. It's through empathy that we build meaningful relationships, offer support, and make a difference in the lives of those around us. I believe in lending a hand to those who need it, offering a listening ear, and creating spaces of comfort for others to heal. This value has also taught me the importance of being kind to myself, especially during times of failure or self-doubt.

3. Lifelong Learning and Growth

Learning does not stop once we finish formal education; it is an ongoing process that continues throughout life. My philosophy centers on continuous growth—intellectually, emotionally, and spiritually. The pursuit of knowledge and personal development is a lifelong journey, and every experience is an opportunity to learn something new. Whether it's through formal education, personal reflection, or professional challenges, I am committed to constantly expanding my horizons. Growth is not just about acquiring skills but also about evolving as a person— becoming more patient, more understanding, and more open-minded.

4. Family and Loyalty

Family is the foundation upon which my life is built. The values instilled in me by my parents—integrity, hard work, and kindness—have been my guiding lights throughout my life. Despite the challenges and losses we have faced, I have always remained committed to my family. I believe in the power of loyalty, not just to those we are related to by blood but to those we choose to call family. Relationships built on trust, respect, and unconditional support are the ones that stand the test of time. My son, Parth, is the living embodiment of my family values, and every step I take is motivated by the desire to give him a life filled with love, security, and opportunity.

5. Integrity and Honesty

Integrity is at the heart of my personal and professional life. I believe in doing what is right, even when it is difficult, and remaining true to my values, regardless of external pressures. Honesty is not just about telling the truth; it is about living authentically, aligning my actions with my words, and holding myself accountable. I believe that integrity is the foundation of all lasting relationships, both personal and professional. Without honesty and trust, no relationship can thrive, and no endeavor can succeed.

6. Giving Back and Social Responsibility

Throughout my life, I have witnessed the power of giving—whether through time, resources, or kindness. I am passionate about giving back to the community, and I firmly believe that success is measured not just by personal achievements but by the impact we have on others. My father's example of generosity and social responsibility has deeply influenced me, and I strive to carry on that legacy. Whether it's through volunteer work, charitable contributions, or simply offering a helping hand, I believe in the importance of contributing to the greater good. We all have a role to play in making the world a better place, and it is our responsibility to use our blessings to uplift others.

7. Gratitude and Contentment

Amidst the hustle and bustle of life, I've learned the importance of gratitude. It is easy to get caught up in what we don't have or what we haven't achieved, but true contentment comes from appreciating the present moment and being thankful for what we have. This philosophy has allowed me to find peace even during the toughest times. I take time every day to reflect on the blessings in my life—my health, my family, my work, and the simple joys of living. Gratitude has taught me that fulfillment doesn't come from material wealth or success, but from being at peace with oneself and one's circumstances.

In the whirlwind of life's responsibilities—whether as a parent, a professional, or a community member— it is easy to neglect our own well-being. However, I have come to understand that self-care is not a luxury but a necessity. Without nurturing our mental, physical, and emotional health, we cannot give our best to others. Finding balance in life—between work and rest, giving and receiving, solitude and connection—has been essential in maintaining my well-being. I believe that we must take time to recharge, reflect, and care for ourselves, so we can continue to show up fully in all aspects of life.

In conclusion, my philosophy and values serve as the bedrock upon which I build my life. They are the principles I hold close, the compass that helps me navigate the complexities of existence. Each day, I strive to live in alignment with these values, not because they are easy, but because they bring meaning and fulfillment to my life. Through resilience, compassion, integrity, and growth, I aim to leave a legacy of kindness, strength, and purpose—one that can inspire others to live a life of impact, authenticity, and love.

Chapter 11

Parth – The Light of My Life

In every mother's life, there is a moment when their heart expands in a way they never thought possible, and for me, that moment came with the birth of my son, Parth. He is not just my child; he is the very essence of my strength, my joy, and my purpose. His arrival marked the beginning of an incredible journey—one filled with love, challenges, growth, and, above all, an unbreakable bond that has shaped my life in ways I never imagined.

When I first found out I was expecting Parth, I was overwhelmed with a mixture of emotions. I was excited, yes, but also filled with uncertainty, especially when the doctors warned me that Parth had arrived prematurely. They said his chances of survival were slim, and those words echoed in my mind, consuming my thoughts with fear and doubt. It was a time of great uncertainty, and I remember holding Parth for the first time, his tiny body so fragile and delicate in my arms, feeling an overwhelming need to protect him at all costs. I could not imagine life without him, and the thought of losing him was a pain I could hardly bear.

But Parth is a fighter. Against all odds, he defied every expectation and fought his way through the early challenges. Watching him grow, overcome obstacles, and flourish has been one of the most rewarding experiences of my life. He has always been a bright light in our home, bringing joy and laughter into even the most difficult days. His presence has been a constant reminder that no matter how hard life gets, there is always hope, and there is always room for love and resilience.

Parth's resilience is something I have always admired. He has faced his own set of challenges growing up, but he has approached them with courage and determination that far surpasses his age. As a mother, I have watched him navigate life with grace, striving to do his best in everything he sets his mind to. I have seen him work tirelessly to achieve his goals, from his academic achievements to his personal growth. Parth's journey through life has been nothing short of inspiring, and I find myself continually in awe of the person he is becoming.

Completing his Bachelor of Journalism & Mass Communication from Amity University, Lucknow, was a milestone that filled me with immense pride. I had always believed in his potential, but seeing him achieve such a significant accomplishment reaffirmed my belief that he is capable of achieving anything he puts his heart and mind to. I remember the long nights of study, the late-night conversations, and the constant support he needed from me, and I was there every step of the way. Watching him graduate was not just a celebration of his academic success, but also a celebration of his perseverance and his commitment to his dreams.

What makes Parth truly special is not just his academic achievements or his accomplishments, but his heart. He is a kind, compassionate, and thoughtful young man who always puts others first. His ability to empathize, listen, and offer support to those around him is a trait that many people admire. He is always the first to help a friend, to comfort someone in need, and to offer words of encouragement. Parth's kindness is one of the many reasons why he is so loved by everyone who knows him, and I am proud every day to be his mother.

I often find myself reflecting on the journey that brought us to this point. I think about the sleepless nights, the countless challenges, and the moments of fear and doubt. But I also think about the love, the laughter, and the pride that Parth has brought into my life. He is my reason for everything, my greatest joy and my unwavering source of strength. Every milestone he reaches, every success he achieves, fills my heart with gratitude and pride. But it is the person he is becoming—the thoughtful, driven, compassionate young man—that fills me with the most pride.

Parth's life has not been easy, but he has made it beautiful. He has shown me the true meaning of resilience, love, and hope. His presence in my life has been a gift, and I am endlessly grateful for the bond we share. As a mother, my greatest wish is for him to continue to follow his heart, to chase his dreams, and to always know that I am here for him, cheering him on every step of the way.

In every sense, Parth is the light of my life. He has illuminated my world with his love, his laughter, and his determination. His journey is far from over, and I have no doubt that he will continue to inspire and touch the lives of those around him. I am proud to be his mother, and I am excited to see the incredible things he will continue to accomplish as he pursues his dreams and builds his own path in this world.

Chapter 12

A Tribute to My Father

There are some figures in our lives who leave an indelible mark, shaping not only the person we are but the person we strive to become. For me, that figure has always been my father. His life, his values, and his unwavering support were the foundation on which I built my own journey. As I reflect on his remarkable legacy, I find myself filled with immense gratitude for the lessons he imparted and the love he so generously gave.

My father was not just a parent; he was a pillar of strength, a source of wisdom, and a beacon of integrity. From a young age, I witnessed his unwavering determination as he worked tirelessly to provide for our family.

His journey as a fragrance designer in an era where the industry was still evolving is nothing short of inspiring. He single-handedly built a thriving business, overcoming countless obstacles along the way. His passion for his craft and his dedication to excellence were qualities that left an everlasting impression on me .what truly set my father apart was not just his professional success, but the man he was at his core. He believed in the power of kindness, humility, and giving back to the community. His generosity knew no bounds, whether it was through supporting local temples, providing shelter for those in need, or simply offering a helping hand to anyone who crossed his path. These values became the cornerstone of our family ethos and a guiding light in my own life.

During the most challenging periods of my life, my father stood by me as a constant source of encouragement and support. When I faced the trials of single parenthood, he stepped in without hesitation, offering not only financial stability but emotional strength. He was not just a grandfather to Parth; he was a role model and a source of endless love and care. The bond between them was beautiful to witness, and I know his influence will forever be etched in Parth's heart as it is in mine.

Beyond his role as a father and grandfather, he was also a mentor and a confidant. He had an incredible ability to listen without judgment, offering advice that was both practical and profound. His wisdom was a blend of experience and intuition, and his words carried the weight of someone who had seen the world, faced its challenges, and emerged stronger.

Losing my father was a loss I can never fully articulate. It felt as though the ground beneath me had shifted, leaving a void that no one else could fill. Yet, even in his absence, his presence continues to guide me. His teachings, his love, and his legacy are woven into the fabric of my life, shaping my decisions and inspiring me to strive for a life of purpose and meaning.

Every time I face a challenge, I think of his resilience. Every time I have an opportunity to help someone, I think of his generosity. And every time I look at Parth, I am reminded of the love and strength that my father embodied so effortlessly.

This chapter of my life is dedicated to him, not just as a tribute to his memory, but as a celebration of everything he stood for. My father was a man who lived with integrity, who loved unconditionally, and who inspired those around him to be their best selves. His impact on my life is immeasurable, and his legacy will forever be a part of who I am.

In his honor, I strive every day to live a life that would make him proud—a life guided by kindness, resilience, and love. He may no longer be with us in person, but his spirit lives on in our hearts, in our actions, and in the values he so lovingly instilled in us. My father was, and always will be, the greatest influence on my life, and for that, I am eternally grateful.

Chapter 13

To the Heart That Raised Me – My Mother

As I reflect on my journey, I can't help but acknowledge the one constant in my life: my mother, Urmila Mehrotra. She has been the backbone of my existence, the quiet strength that has carried me through the most challenging times. No matter how difficult life became, she always stood by me with a calm and unshakable support that I never truly understood until I grew older.

There were countless moments when the weight of the world felt too heavy, when I doubted myself and questioned if I could continue. During those times, my mother's wisdom and unwavering belief in me gave me the courage to keep going. She never asked for anything in return. Her love was a constant, unconditional force that shaped me into who I am today. Whether it was managing my struggles, comforting me during my failures, or guiding me toward my successes, she was always there—selflessly putting my needs before her own.

She taught me that strength isn't always loud or flashy; sometimes, it's the quiet, determined persistence to never give up. She faced the hardest moments of life with a grace I now strive to embody, never letting me feel the burden of her sacrifices. Her ability to balance so much while making sure I never lacked love or care was nothing short of extraordinary.

I've come to understand that a mother's love is a quiet but powerful force—one that shapes a child's life in ways they may not even realize at the time. As I look back on my journey, I recognize just how much of her spirit lives within me. My mother didn't just raise me; she crafted the foundation upon which my dreams were built, all while providing me with a sense of security and love that allowed me to go after those dreams.

I owe so much of my journey to her strength, wisdom, and the quiet way she managed both my struggles and her own. She was, and continues to be, the unsung hero of my life, the one who always knew exactly what I needed— whether it was a word of encouragement, a hand to hold, or the tough love that pushed me forward when I wanted to stop.

In the chapters of my life, the one constant has been her unwavering support. Her influence has shaped me into who I am, and as I continue on this journey, I carry with me the lessons she imparted, the love she gave, and the strength she showed

#AMAN&TANAYAFO

BEGINNING OF NEW CHAPTER

Chapter 14

My Journey

Life has always been unpredictable, but its beauty lies in its ability to surprise us with strength we never knew we had. As I sit down to pen this chapter, I can't help but reflect on my journey so far—a journey that has tested me, shaped me, and transformed me into the person I am today. From 2002 to 2024, my life has been a rollercoaster of struggles, sacrifices, and self-discovery. Yet, amidst it all, I've found moments of hope, love, and courage that have carried me forward.

My story took a dramatic turn with the birth of my son. What should have been a moment of pure joy became a turning point that tested my resilience. My husband left us shortly after his birth, leaving me to navigate the challenges of single parenthood. It was a devastating blow, one that shattered my sense of stability and forced me to question everything I had envisioned for my future. But in those darkest moments, I made a promise to myself and my newborn child—that I would give him the best life possible, no matter the cost.

Raising my son as a single parent has been both my greatest challenge and my proudest achievement. From his first steps to his first day of school, I have been there for him every step of the way. I managed his schooling, his extracurricular activities, and his upbringing, ensuring that he never felt the absence of a father. Every success he achieved felt like a triumph for both of us, a testament to the love and determination that fueled our little family. My parents played a crucial role during this time, stepping in as my pillars of support. Their love and guidance gave me the strength to keep going, even when the road ahead seemed uncertain.

But life was not just about raising my son—it was also about rediscovering myself. Education has always been a cornerstone of my identity.

Even after graduation, I didn't stop learning. I pursued professional courses, including Aptake, to enhance my skills and broaden my horizons. These certifications not only added value to my career but also gave me a sense of personal fulfillment. Each milestone I achieved was a reminder that it's never too late to chase your dreams, no matter how many obstacles stand in your way. Currently,

I am pursuing an MBA from Amity University, a step that I believe will open new doors of opportunity for me. The decision to go back to school while managing my responsibilities as a mother was daunting, but it was also empowering. Every class I attend, every assignment I submit, is a step toward a brighter future for both myself and my son.

Throughout this journey, my parents have been my unwavering support system. They stepped in to help with my son whenever I needed time to study or work, ensuring that I never felt alone in this journey. Their faith in me gave me the confidence to push forward, even when the odds seemed stacked against me. Their love and encouragement have been the wind beneath my wings, allowing me to soar higher than I ever thought possible.

But it wasn't just about surviving—it was about thriving. Over the years, I've learned to embrace the challenges as opportunities for growth. The struggles I faced taught me resilience and the importance of believing in myself. There were moments of doubt, of course—times when I questioned whether I was doing enough, whether I was strong enough. But every time I looked at my son, I found my answer. His smile, his achievements, and his unwavering trust in me were all the motivation I needed to keep going.

Being a single parent has also taught me the importance of self-reliance. I learned to manage finances, make tough decisions, and create a stable environment for my son. These experiences have shaped me into a stronger, more independent person. They've also shown me the power of love and determination. When you have a purpose, when you're fighting for something bigger than yourself, you discover strength you never knew you had.

Looking back, I can see how far I've come. The girl who once felt lost and broken has grown into a woman who is confident, resilient, and ready to take on whatever comes next. My journey has been anything but easy, but it has been worth every tear, every sleepless night, and every sacrifice. It has taught me that life is not about waiting for the storm to pass—it's about learning to dance in the rain.

As I turn the page to this new chapter, I carry with me the lessons of the past and the hopes of the future. This is not just a beginning—it's a celebration of everything I've overcome and everything I'm yet to achieve. I am excited to embrace new opportunities, to continue learning and growing, and to build a life that reflects the values I hold dear. Most importantly, I am committed to being the best mother, daughter, and person I can be.

This chapter is not just about me—it's about the people who have stood by me, the dreams I've dared to dream, and the future I am determined to create. It is a reminder that no matter how difficult the journey, every step is a testament to our strength, our resilience, and our ability to rise above. And as I move forward, I do so with a heart full of gratitude, a mind full of dreams, and a spirit that refuses to give up.

Chapter 15

The Strength of My Journey – Parth

Parth is not just my son; he is my greatest source of strength and a constant reminder of the beauty and resilience of life. At 22 years old, he has already achieved so much, and his journey is nothing short of inspiring. From his early years to now, Parth has been a shining light in my life, not only as my child but also as my unwavering supporter.

Parth's schooling began at *Millennium School,* where he was known for his cheerful personality and eagerness to learn. Watching him grow and flourish in those formative years was one of my greatest joys. Despite the challenges that life threw our way, Parth always approached his studies and life with determination and a positive spirit. His teachers often praised his hard work, and his classmates admired his friendly nature.

After completing his schooling, Parth pursued his graduation from *Amity University*, a milestone that filled me with immense pride. Throughout his academic journey, he displayed a level of dedication and focus that inspired not just me but everyone around him. Managing his studies and personal growth while also offering me emotional support was a testament to his strong character and maturity.

Parth's hobbies have always been a big part of who he is, and cricket holds a special place in his heart. Watching him play on the field, full of energy and enthusiasm, is a sight that

always brings a smile to my face. His love for the game goes beyond just playing—it's a passion that drives him, teaching him lessons in teamwork, patience, and perseverance. His favorite cricketer, Rohit Sharma, is someone he admires deeply, not just for his skill but for his sportsmanship and ability to rise above challenges.

One of the most defining aspects of Parth's journey has been his hearing impairment. Diagnosed at a young age, he faced difficulties that most people couldn't even imagine. But Parth never let this define him. He underwent a cochlear implant, a small, complex electronic device that provides a sense of sound to those who are profoundly deaf or severely hard-of-hearing. The implant, consisting of an external portion behind the ear and a surgically placed internal component, transformed his life, enabling him to hear and engage with the world in ways that were previously out of reach.

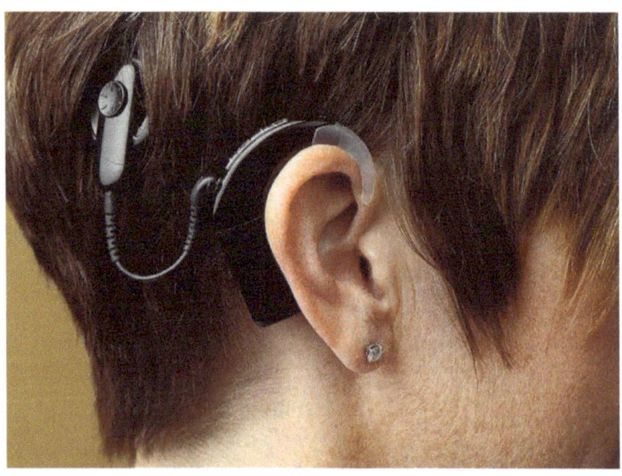

Parth's journey with the cochlear implant was not an easy one. It required countless hours of therapy, adjustments, and immense patience. But his determination to overcome this challenge was truly remarkable. He adapted to the device with grace and worked tirelessly to ensure it didn't hold him back from achieving his dreams. His resilience in the face of this challenge has been a source of inspiration for everyone who knows him.

What makes Parth truly special is his kind and supportive nature. Despite his own struggles, he has always been my rock. From a young age, he understood the sacrifices I made for him and reciprocated with unconditional love and encouragement. Whether it was helping me around the house, being my cheerleader during my studies, or simply offering a comforting word when I was feeling overwhelmed, Parth has always been there for me.

Parth's ability to empathize and connect with others is one of his most admirable qualities. He never hesitates to lend a helping hand or offer a word of encouragement to those in need. His presence in my life has been a constant reminder that love and support can move mountains, and I am endlessly grateful for the bond we share.

Today, as I look at the young man Parth has become, I am filled with pride and gratitude. He has faced life's challenges with courage, pursued his dreams with passion, and supported me with unwavering dedication. Parth is not just my son; he is my partner in this journey, and his strength and positivity continue to inspire me every single day.

Chapter 16

Hearing Journey of Path

Parth's journey through life was extraordinary from the very beginning. Born with a unique challenge, his hearing disparity set him apart from other children his age. What seemed like a simple developmental delay in infancy turned out to be a significant hurdle that shaped the course of his life. Parth's story is one of resilience, determination, and the unwavering belief that he could achieve greatness despite the odds stacked against him. Early Diagnosis and Initial Struggles Parth's parents first noticed signs of hearing difficulties when he was a toddler. Unlike other children, he would not respond to his name or turn towards sounds. Concerned, his parents consulted pediatricians, who recommended a battery of tests to determine the cause of his auditory challenges. The tests began with BETA (Brainstem Evoked Response Audiometry) tests, which evaluated the auditory nerve pathways. This was followed by OAE (Otoacoustic Emissions) tests, designed to assess the functionality of the cochlea, the inner ear's sensory organ. These tests confirmed the diagnosis: Parth had significant hearing loss. The news was devastating for the family, but they refused to let it define Parth's future. Specialists recommended regressive therapies to stimulate his auditory system and train his brain to process sound more effectively. These therapies were intense and required immense patience from both Parth and his caregivers. For hours each day, he underwent exercises designed to enhance his auditory perception and speech clarity. The process was grueling, often leaving him exhausted, but his determination shone through. The Role of Advanced Healthcare Parth's case caught the attention of major multinational corporations (MNCs) specializing in healthcare innovation. Recognizing the potential for advancements in his treatment, these companies collaborated to provide cutting-edge solutions. Parth was fitted with state-of-the-art hearing aids that amplified sound frequencies tailored to his specific needs. These devices became his constant companions, opening a world of sound that he had never fully experienced before. Additionally, Parth's treatment included access to advanced auditory-verbal therapies. Specialists worked tirelessly to help him adapt to his new reality. These sessions were not just about improving his hearing but also focused on integrating him into a world dominated by sound. Through consistent support from healthcare professionals and his family, Parth began to make progress. Overcoming Educational Challenges Entering the world of education presented another set of challenges for Parth. Unlike other children, he had to navigate classrooms filled with ambient noise, deciphering instructions through a mix of lip-reading, auditory cues, and visual aids. Initially, teachers were hesitant, unsure of how to accommodate his unique needs. However, Parth's tenacity quickly changed their perspective. He approached learning with an eagerness that was impossible to ignore. My family worked closely with educators to create an environment conducive to his learning. They ensured he sat in the front row to minimize distractions and maximize his ability to hear the teacher. They also advocated for the use of technology, such as FM systems, which transmitted the teacher's voice directly to his hearing aids. These accommodations, coupled with Parth's relentless effort, allowed him to thrive academically. Despite these adjustments, there were moments of frustration. Social interactions with peers were sometimes strained due to communication barriers. Yet, Parth's resilience and warm personality won him friends who supported and encouraged him. Over time, he learned to navigate these challenges with grace, proving that he could excel in both academics and relationships. The Emotional Toll Behind Parth's success was a silent struggle that often went unnoticed. The emotional toll of his journey was immense. There were days when the weight of his challenges felt overwhelming, and the fear of being left behind loomed large. Yet, my family became his anchor during these difficult times. the unwavering belief in his abilities provided him with the strength to persevere. My mother was a pillar of support for the parth. She devoted herself entirely to his well-being, attending every therapy session, consulting with specialists, and advocating for his needs. Her love and determination were instrumental in shaping Parth's journey. She often reminded him that his hearing disparity was not a limitation but a unique aspect of his identity that he could embrace. Achieving Milestones Parth's journey was marked by significant milestones that showcased his incredible progress. Despite the rigorous demands of therapy and education, he excelled academically, earning degrees that many believed were out of reach. Each achievement was a testament to his hard work and the support system that stood firmly by his side. Graduating from high school was a particularly emotional moment for Parth and the family. It

symbolized not just academic success but also the triumph of determination over adversity. A cochlear implant is a groundbreaking medical device designed to help individuals with severe hearing loss or deafness regain the ability to hear. Unlike hearing aids, which amplify sound, a cochlear implant works by bypassing the damaged parts of the ear and directly stimulating the auditory nerve. The device consists of two main parts an external microphone and speech processor that captures sound, and an internal component that is surgically implanted under the skin behind the ear. The sound is then converted into electrical signals, which are sent to the brain, enabling the person to perceive sound.

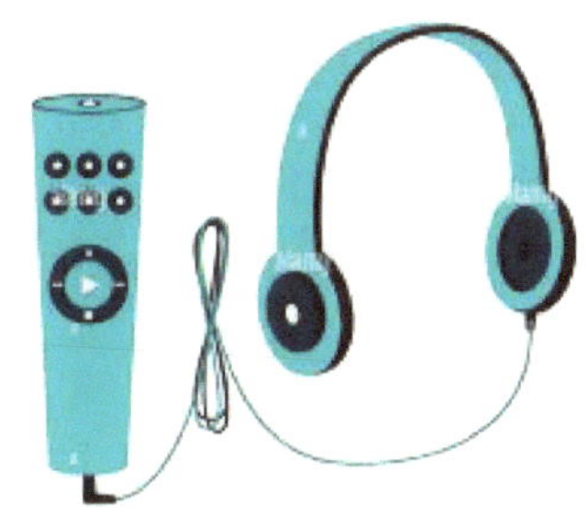

Cochlear implants can provide significant improvement in hearing and speech understanding for those who have not benefited from conventional hearing aids, offering a new world of auditory experiences for people with profound hearing loss. The success of cochlear implants often depends on factors such as age, the duration of hearing loss, and the individual's commitment to therapy and rehabilitation. Parth went on to pursue higher education, earning degrees in fields that required immense focus and dedication. His ability to adapt and excel in these environments left a lasting impression on everyone who crossed his path. Inspiring Others Parth's story became a source of inspiration for many. His journey demonstrated that with resilience and the right support, no challenge is insurmountable. A Life Beyond Challenges Today, Parth stands as a beacon of hope and perseverance. He has not only achieved academic and professional success but has also embraced his journey as a vital part of his identity. His story is a reminder that life's challenges, no matter how daunting, can be overcome with courage, determination, and the support of those who believe in us. Parth's hearing journey is more than a tale of struggle; it is a celebration of the human spirit's ability to rise above adversity. His life continues to inspire those around him, proving that with the right mindset, anything is possible. As Parth often says, "The sound of success is sweetest when it's heard through the echoes of perseverance."

Chapter 17

A Mother's Fight

In a small corner of a vast forest, there lived a female bird named Lyra. She was young, vibrant, and full of life, fluttering through the trees with grace. One sunny morning, she met a male bird, Orion, whose feathers shimmered with a brilliant hue. The two shared many joyful moments, their songs echoing through the forest as they built a nest together. But soon after, Lyra gave birth to their baby bird, a tiny, fragile creature who needed care and warmth.

As the days passed, something unexpected happened. Orion, the father, left. Perhaps the winds called him, or perhaps the freedom of the skies pulled him away, but he flew off, leaving Lyra alone with the baby. The forest was vast, and the days felt longer without the companionship of Orion.

But Lyra, despite her heartbreak, didn't falter. The survival of her baby depended on her, and she knew that. With unwavering determination, she spread her wings and took to the skies alone. The forest, once full of joy with the sounds of both birds singing together, now felt a little emptier. But Lyra was strong, and she had to be.

Every day, she worked tirelessly to gather food. She fluttered from tree to tree, searching for the juiciest berries, the tastiest insects, and the seeds that could nourish her and her baby. It wasn't easy. The forest, which once seemed so welcoming, was now filled with dangers. There were predators that lurked, and storms that could come at any moment. Lyra had to be cautious and resourceful, keeping her baby safe from the dangers of the world while finding enough to eat.

As days turned into weeks, Lyra's journey of motherhood became more challenging. She had to build a secure nest with twigs, leaves, and soft moss. She made sure her home was safe, far from any danger, so that her baby could grow strong. She spent hours arranging everything perfectly, always watching over her little one with a watchful eye. But perhaps the greatest challenge was the endless feeding. Every morning, Lyra would forage for food, returning to the nest with what she could find. Her baby chirped for food, eager to grow and explore the world outside the nest. Lyra would feed him tirelessly, ensuring he had the strength to fly when the time came. But even as her wings grew weary from the endless search for food, her love for her baby never wavered.

The storms came, and the winds howled, but Lyra stood firm. There were nights when the rain poured, but she kept her baby warm beneath her wings, protecting him from the cold. She had learned to navigate through the harshest of times, with a fierce determination that came from the love she felt for her young one.

Through the struggles, Lyra grew stronger. The challenges she faced, the loneliness she endured, and the hardships she overcame, only made her more resilient. And as the day finally came when her baby learned to fly, she knew that all her efforts had not been in vain. Her baby soared high into the sky, ready to face the world, and Lyra watched with pride.

In her journey as a mother, Lyra had not only created a home, but had also built the strength to face life's challenges alone. She understood now that even in the most difficult of times, one can find the strength to keep moving forward. Much like her, you too can weather the storms and emerge stronger, knowing that your journey is one of resilience, love, and unwavering determination.

This story, though of a bird, mirrors my own journey. It's a reflection of the times I faced struggles, the challenges I encountered when the path seemed uncertain, and the strength I found within myself to push forward. Through every difficulty, I've learned that, just like Lyra, I can build a life, face my fears, and rise above whatever comes my way.

By- Archana Mehrotra

Chapter 18

Looking Ahead

As I turn the pages of my life's story, I find myself standing at a crossroads of reflection and aspiration. Each chapter has been a blend of trials and triumphs, of growth and gratitude. But as I look ahead, I am filled with hope, determination, and a deep sense of purpose for what the future holds.

Life has been a constant teacher, showing me the value of resilience, the strength in vulnerability, and the importance of embracing change. The journey I have traveled so far has shaped me into the person I am today—a person who is not afraid to dream, to evolve, and to keep moving forward. Looking ahead, I am not just focused on personal milestones but also on the legacy I wish to leave behind for the people I love and the communities I serve.

One of my foremost aspirations is to continue being a guiding force for Parth. Watching him grow into a compassionate and accomplished individual has been one of my greatest joys. As he charts his own course in life, my role as his mother shifts from being a nurturer to a mentor and a friend. I aim to support his dreams, encourage his ambitions, and remind him of the values that have been the foundation of our family.

Professionally, I see the future as a canvas of possibilities. The lessons I have learned from my father's entrepreneurial spirit and my own experiences have instilled in me a passion for creativity, innovation, and hard work. Whether through my writing, my contributions to the community, or new ventures I embark upon, I want to make a meaningful impact in everything I do. The pursuit of lifelong learning continues to drive me, and I am committed to honing my skills, exploring new opportunities, and challenging myself to grow in ways I never imagined.

On a personal level, I envision a life rich with connections, experiences, and fulfillment. Relationships and friendships have always been an integral part of my journey, and I look forward to nurturing these bonds further. Surrounding myself with people who inspire, support, and uplift me has been a source of immense strength, and I am grateful for the love that have graced my life.

Beyond my immediate circle, my heart remains deeply connected to the causes that resonate with me. Giving back to society is not just a responsibility but a privilege. My father's legacy of kindness and generosity serves as a constant reminder to extend a helping hand to those in need. As I move forward, I am committed to continuing his tradition of community service, whether through charitable initiatives, mentorship, or simply being a source of comfort to someone who needs.

Looking ahead also means embracing change with open arms. Life is unpredictable, and while uncertainty can be daunting, it is also filled with opportunities for transformation. I have learned that growth often comes from stepping outside of our comfort zones and facing challenges head-on. As I navigate the unknowns of the future,

I carry with me the lessons of the past and the unwavering belief that every experience—good or bad—has its purpose.

As I write this final chapter, I am reminded that life is not about reaching a destination but about savoring the journey. Every moment is a gift, and every day is an opportunity to create something beautiful. My story is far from over, and I am excited to see how the chapters ahead unfold. Currently I have enrolled myself for a profession course on entrepreneurship from **IIT DELHI.**

With hope in my heart and determination in my spirit, I look forward to embracing the future with courage, gratitude, and an unwavering commitment to living a life of purpose and love.

Expressions of Gratitude

Life's journey is a tapestry woven with the support, guidance, and love of countless individuals. Reflecting on the chapters of my life, I am deeply grateful to those who have been instrumental in shaping my story and supporting Parth and me through every challenge and triumph.

I would like to express my heartfelt thanks and deep gratitude to Ashutosh Mehrotra for offering invaluable guidance regarding funds and for his expert assistance in managing them. Your support has played a crucial role in helping me navigate financial decisions with confidence. I truly appreciate your expertise and mentorship.

Dr. Arpan Kumar and Dr. Ahmad, your expertise as occupational therapists during Parth's left-hand treatment was a beacon of hope. Dr. Manjula Goswami, your guidance at The Millennium School in Lucknow played a pivotal role in Parth's schooling. I extend my heartfelt gratitude to Akhil Sir, Vidhi Tekwani, Euro Kids, Kidzee, Rajkumar Academy

Lucknow, G.D. Goenka Delhi, and Amity University Lucknow for the academic foundation and nurturing environment you provided to Parth. Special thanks to Dr. Sanjay M. Johri, Head of the Department at Amity University, for your unwavering support during Parth's educational journey.

To Mrs. Kavita Mathur and Mathur Radios, thank you for encouraging Parth's love for poetry and supporting him during his early years. Nitin Arora, your dedication as a photographer and mentor has beautifully documented Parth's dreams and aspirations. The expertise of Dr. Milind Kirtiney, the renowned ENT surgeon at Hinduja Hospital in Mumbai, and Dr. Rajesh Patadia, the audiologist at Hinduja Hospital, was invaluable in Parth's journey of recovery and growth.

I am profoundly thankful to IKMG Chairman Raj Khanna, whose platform has fostered connections and strengthened bonds within the Khattri community. Pandit Rama Shankar Mishra (Gullu Painter) and Pandit Balwant Bhau Shastri Patwardhan, your wisdom and spiritual guidance have enriched my life immeasurably.

Special gratitude goes to Priyanshu Mishra, Nandan Malviya, Prashant Malviya, and my genuine sister who has tirelessly supported me through Aseem Creation. Your presence has been my source of strength and inspiration. To Dinkar Pandey, my music teacher, and Shiv Shankar Pandey, thank you for enriching my life with the joy of music.

Institutions like Wharton University and OCP Academy, where I pursued my post-graduate diploma in digital marketing, have been instrumental in my personal growth, while my journey of learning French continues to inspire me. I am equally grateful to Praveen Mishra of Webdeb, whose professional expertise has supported my endeavors.

In acknowledging the collective influence of these incredible individuals, I recognize that their guidance, compassion, and belief in us have been the cornerstone of our resilience and success. Their contributions have illuminated our path, and for this, I am eternally grateful.

As I look ahead, I carry each of you with me—in my heart, in my thoughts, and in the values I uphold. Together, we have built a story of courage, love, and gratitude, and for that, I am profoundly blessed.

CONTACT DETAILS

Instagram : https://www.instagram.com/archana2013/

Youtube : www.youtube.com/@archanamehrotra2361

Website : https://www.archanamehrotra.in/

Facebook : https://www.facebook.com/people/Archana-Mehrotra/100070310829966/

E-Mail : peridot578@gmail.com

Please scan this QR code to shop for the Kindle edition.